AMZ 9.99

Artificial Flies and How To Make Them
A Book on FlyTying for Fly Fishing

by M.A. Shipley

with an introduction by Roger Chambers

This work contains material that was originally published in 1888.

This publication was created and published for the public benefit, utilizing public funding and is within the Public Domain.

This edition is reprinted for educational purposes and in accordance with all applicable Federal Laws.

Introduction Copyright 2017 by Roger Chambers

Self Reliance Books

Get more historic titles on animal and stock breeding, gardening and old fashioned skills by visiting us at:

http://selfreliancebooks.blogspot.com/

Introduction

I am pleased to present yet another title on Fishing and Fly-tying.

This volume is entitled "Artificial Flies and How To Make Them" and was published in 1888.

The work is in the Public Domain and is re-printed here in accordance with Federal Laws.

As with all reprinted books of this age that are intended to perfectly reproduce the original edition, considerable pains and effort had to be undertaken to correct fading and sometimes outright damage to existing proofs of this title. At times, this task is quite monumental, requiring an almost total "rebuilding" of some pages from digital proofs of multiple copies. Despite this, imperfections still sometimes exist in the final proof and may detract from the visual appearance of the text.

I hope you enjoy reading this book as much as I enjoyed making it available to readers again.

Roger Chambers

The Art of Fly Making.

FLY-making is an art which dates back long before the time of Isaac Walton, who is the patron saint of all anglers, and is both profitable, amusing and entertaining, besides affording that pleasure which comes from being able to catch fish with a lure which you have made yourself.

This short treatise is not intended to be at all exhaustive, but to give some plain, practical directions for tying the flies usually used, which when thoroughly mastered, salmon and other intricate flies can be tied almost by intuition, and I would remark, before commencing, to the would-be learner, do not be discouraged with your first flies. Remember that trout and bass do not look closely to see if a fly is handsomely made or not, and I have seen artificial flies which for appearance were anything but neatly made, take fish as well as others which were everything that could be desired.

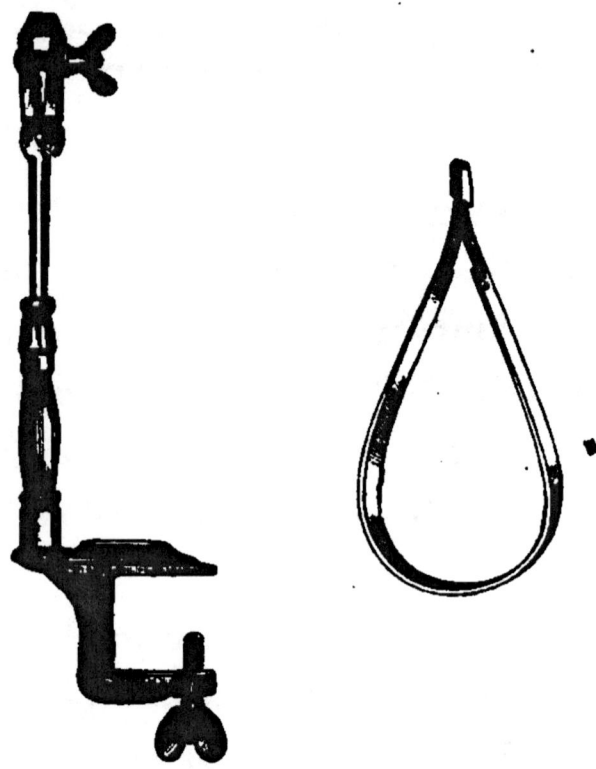

The implements used in fly tying, are a pair of sharp pointed embroidery scissors of fine quality, or better still, a pair with curved blades, a stilletto, a vise, either plain or with an attachment for screwing it to the table (like cut,) and a pair of spring plyers. We would strongly urge our readers to learn to make their flies without the aid of the vise, as we firmly believe they can be made better and stronger and more quickly without its aid, with the possible exception of *intricate salmon* flies.

HACKLE FLIES.

We will first take up the hackle flies, as they are the most simple in construction. Select first the hook, which for making a neat fly must always have a taper shank. The most approved patterns for fly tying are the Sproat and Limerick, but for Hackle and Palmer flies many persons use what is known as the Sneck Bent, and we think with good reason, as any hook without a side bend, if placed between the leaves of a book—which will represent for our purpose the mouth of a fish—you will notice, can readily be withdrawn without the point entering. Now if a hook like the sneck bent be so placed, it cannot be removed without catching on one of the sides.

Select a brown hackle, a piece of peacock

herl, from which cut for a trout fly four strands close to the quill, and a piece of gold tinsel three inches long, and snooding silk twelve or fifteen inches long, which must be well waxed with snooding wax by drawing the silk over it two or three times.

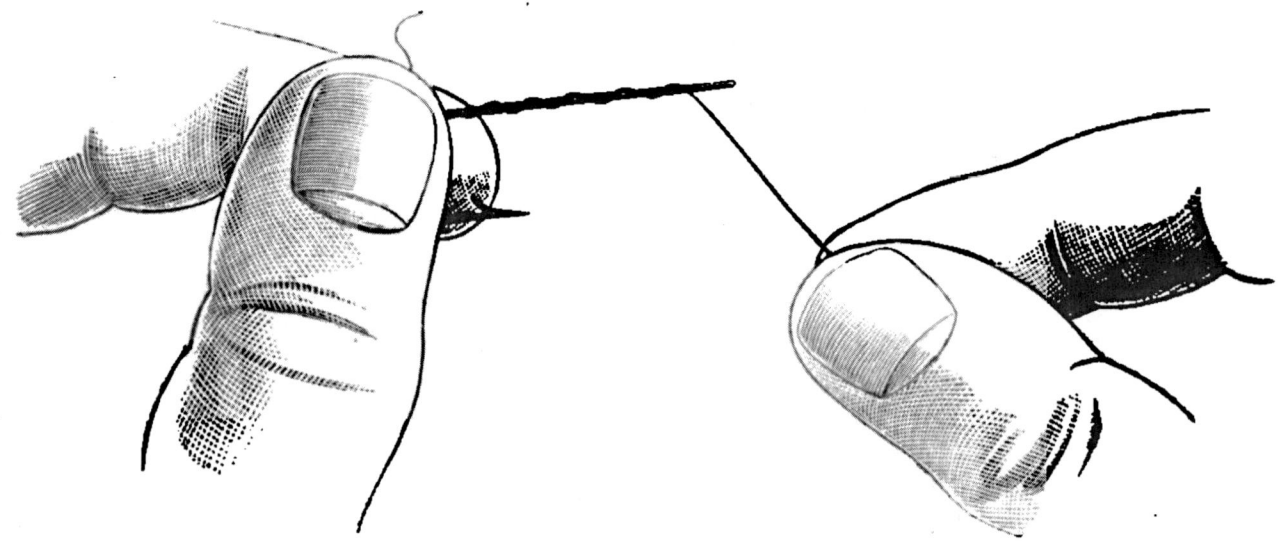

Next select a perfectly clear and round strand of silk worm gut, and having soaked it for five or ten minutes in warm water, tie a loop in one end and cut off the lower part, so as to make it five inches long. Take the hook by the bend, holding it either in the vise or between the thumb and first finger of the left hand, (see cut) wind the wrapping silk spirally around the shank of the hook, the turns being about one-eighth of an inch apart, commencing opposite the point and winding to within one-eighth of an inch of the end, always winding the silk, and in fact everything that is wound on the hook *from* you. Now lay the gut on top and wind closely and firmly down to where you commenced.

Place the piece of gold tinsel on top of the hook, allowing the loose end to lie between the thumb and finger of the left hand, having but one-quarter of an inch of the tinsel on the hook. Take two turns of silk around it one-quarter inch from its end, and at a point on the hook midway between the barb and the point, (see cut) wind the silk loosely around the shank of the hook, continuing up the gut to get it out of your way.

Wrap the tinsel over and over five or six turns around the shank of the hook between the barb and point, catch the loose end with the plyers and let it hang. Unwind the tying silk and fasten the tinsel with three turns of the silk and cut off the surplus tinsel.

Then tie in the herl at its point over the fastening of the tinsel with three turns of silk, after you have previously bunched and drawn them between your thumb and finger from the point to the butt to make it bushy. Now twist the herl and tying silk together with a rolling motion between thumb and finger, (this gives strength to the herl), and carefully wind around the shank of the hook, commencing at the upper portion of the tinsel and wrapping up to within one-quarter of an inch of the end of the hook. Untwist the silk from the loose ends of the herl, catch the latter with the plyers and let them hang down; then wind over the herl three or four turns of the winding silk and cut off the surplus herl close to the wrapping.

Take the hackle which you have selected, by

THE ART OF FLY TYING.

the extreme point with the left hand, and stroke back the fibres with the thumb and finger of the right, by drawing it between them; (see cut) now with your scissors cut from the point two or three hairs on each side; next lay the point

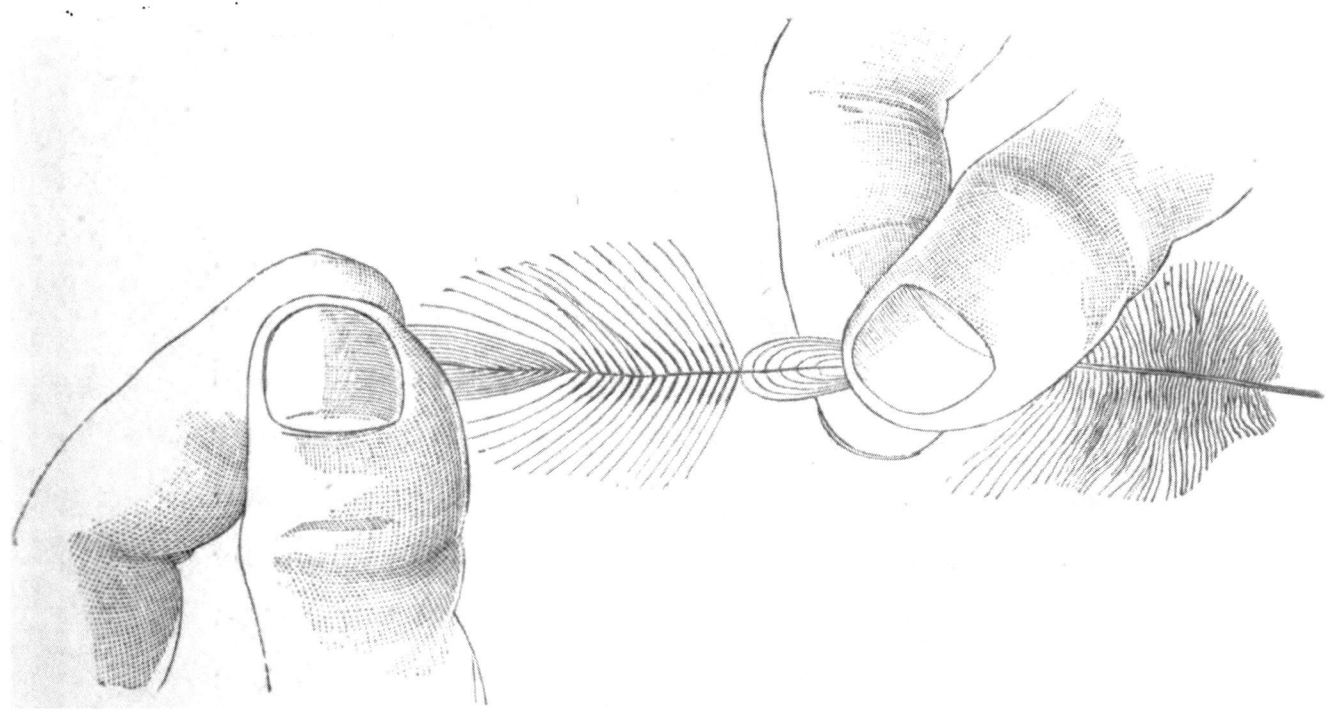

underside down on top of the hook and over the place where you tied in the herl, and tie it on also with three or four turns of the silk, (see cut on page 10.) Cut off the *point* left over after it is tied, and catch the quill of the hackle in the plyers and twist the wrapping silk loosely around the gut. Wind the hackle around the hook continuously up to within one thirty-second of an inch of

the end of the hook, being careful not to wrap over the turns already on; let the plyers hang and wind two turns of silk around the hackle and hook. Now take the stilletto and pick out any fibres of hackle which you may have wrapped over. In winding on the hackle, care should be taken not to twist it, but wind it on edgeways with the underside of the feather toward the point of the hook. Cut off the end of the hackle by snipping the *quill only* close to the winding. Stroke back the fibres at the head of the fly toward the tail, and hold them down with the thumb and finger of the left hand, and wind over them at the root of the hackle of the last turn of the feather three turns of silk, then lay a loop in your silk by placing the loose end on the gut three inches above the hook, and wind around the gut *inside* of the loop thus formed, four turns of the silk, winding it the *reverse* of the way you wrapped it around the hook in making the fly. Now lay the loose end of the silk along the side of the fly, catch the silk by the loop and wind it around the head of the

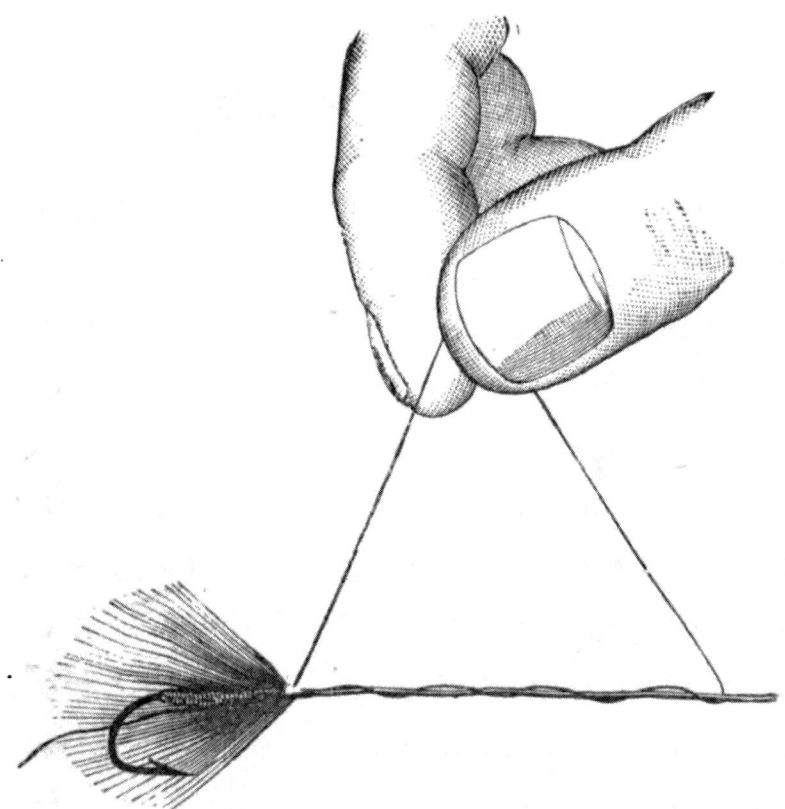

INVISIBLE KNOT.

fly and over the end of the silk on its side, this will undo the turns around the gut, when you can catch hold of the loose end and pull it tight, thus making an invisible knot and a small head, which is a great desideratum in fly tying. (See cut.)

Now varnish the silk wrapping on the head by using a pointed stick dipped into shellac varnish, and the fly is complete.

SILK BODY HACKLE FLIES.

For silk body flies proceed exactly the same as in the description for a herl body, until you come to tying in the herl, in place of which cut off four to five inches of embroidery or floss silk. If of the former, make it into two lengths by untwisting it, and tie in the two ends thus formed on top of the tinsel. Wind your tying silk up out of the way, catch hold of the silk for the body, and without twisting it wind it over and over around the shank of the hook to within one-quarter of an inch of the end, making it larger in the centre and a gradual taper towards the head and tail. Catch hold of it with the plyers, let them hang and fasten it off with three turns of your wrapping silk, and cut off the surplus body close to the wrapping. Now proceed with your hackle exactly the same as in the herl body.

MOHAIR OR WOOL BODIES.

Some insects can be best imitated with mohair or wool bodies, notably flies of the caterpillar order, like Palmers and Hackles, and the cow dung in the winged flies. To make these you will find crewel—a material used for embroidery—very satisfactory, as it can be procured in almost any shade of color desired. Cut and untwist it the same as you were instructed to do in making silk bodies. It can then be wrapped on in exactly the same manner as the silk, or if you use the crude mohair, which at times is preferable, on account of being able to more nearly match the color of an insect, as two or more colors can be mixed to form a body. As for instance, a yellow and green to make a greenish yellow. Pull from the bunch a small quantity and roll it between your hands. Our object in this is to make it larger in the centre and a gradual taper toward each end, thus when wrapped on, giving the swell to the body of the fly which so much improves its appearance. This is wrapped around the hook the same as a silk body, with the exception that —unlike silk—as it is wrapped it requires to be slightly twisted to give strength to the fibres, while wrapping otherwise it is liable to pull apart. For small flies, such as gnats and midges, this body is often used without any hackle, and the legs of the fly which the hackle represents are picked out with a stilletto at the head after the fly is made.

PALMER FLIES.

We will now take up the Palmer fly. The difference between what is known as a Palmer and a Hackle fly is that in the former the

PALMER FLY.

hackle is tied in at the tail of the fly and is wound around the body as well as at the head. In the latter, the hackle is wound on at the head only. Select the materials and wind on the gut precisely the same as directed for making the brown hackle, except in this instance we will make a black Palmer, which requires a black body, and is wrapped with silver tinsel. After the gut is snooded or wrapped on to the hook, select your hackle and press back the fibres, (see cut, page 9) and cut a few hairs from each side of its point. Let it lie over the left hand between the thumb and finger, tie the point in *underside* down, at a place midway between the point and the barb of the hook. Cut off a piece of tinsel four inches long and tie in one end over the tying of the hackle, allowing the loose end to lie back over your left hand, then cut off a piece of silk three to five inches long, (depending on size of hook you are using) and untwist it, making it into two lengths; tie in the two ends thus made

over where you tied in your hackle. (See cut). Now wind your tying silk up the gut loosely out of the way, catch hold of the loose end of the silk from which you are to make the body, and *without twisting it*, wind it over and over around the shank of the hook, to within one-quarter of an inch of the end of the hook, making it larger in the centre, with a gradual taper towards the head and tail. Catch hold of the surplus silk with the plyers and let them hang; fasten it with three turns of the tying silk, and cut off the remainder close to the wrapping. Wrap your tying silk around the gut as before, catch hold of the loose end of the tinsel with the plyers and wrap it first four turns around the shank of the hook immediately below the body and underneath the hackle, and then spirally up and around the body, allowing the turns to be about one thirty-second of an inch or the width of the tinsel apart. Finish off where you tied off the body one-quarter inch from end of hook and cut off the surplus tinsel. Wind the tying silk around the gut as before, catch hold of the end of the hackle by its quill with the plyers, and wind it spirally edgeways around the body of the fly between the wrappings of the tinsel, underside of the feather toward the point of the hook, up to where you have tied in your body, where it must be wound *closely* three or four times, taking care not to wrap over the turns already on. Let the plyers hang and finish off in the same manner as directed in making a hackle fly.

The hackle and Palmer flies are excellent trout and bass lures, and are tied in various colored bodies and hackles. In making Palmer flies for *bass*, the bodies should be made large and full and the hackles very bushy; and frequently it is necessary, in order to do this, to tie in two hackles in place of one, and wind on both together; or tie in the first hackle and wind it up to the end of the body only and finish it off, then select another hackle and tie it in where you finished off the first hackle in the reverse of the way hackles are usually tied, *i. e.*, tie in the quill and wind it on and finish as before.

WINGED FLIES.

These generally are of two kinds, the straight and the reverse wing. The former, in our opinion, if well put on, are fully equal in wearing qualities to the reverse wing, while in appearance are more desirable, as they can be made with a much smaller head.

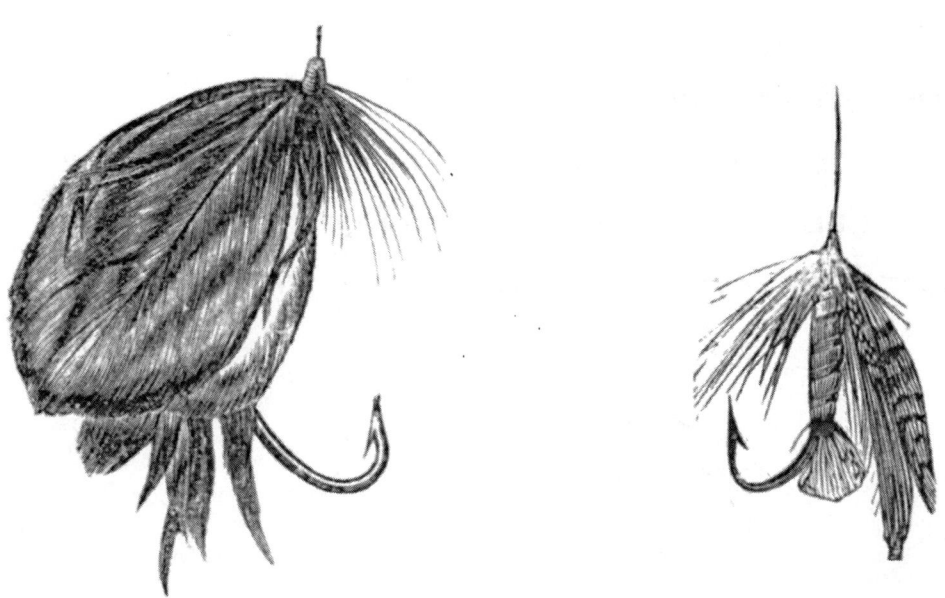

Suppose we desire to make the Queen of the Waters. We select a piece of orange silk, a brown hackle, a piece of gold tinsel, and a mottled feather from the breast of the mallard duck, and proceed exactly as we would for making a Palmer fly, always leaving one-sixteenth of an inch of the hook bare at the head in the making of a winged fly to tie the wing on, as it will be firmer and more secure and make a smaller head than if it were tied around the fastening of the hackle. Now take the mallard feather and hold it between the thumb and finger of the left hand by its point, and draw the fibres back from the point towards the quill until the side of the feather is square or parallel, and each fibre is at a right angle to the quill; on doing this properly depends largely the appearance of the fly after

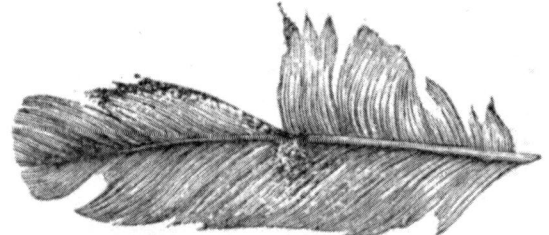

it is finished. (See cut.) If you will examine a feather with the microscope you will find each and every fibre contains hooks on each of its sides which lock into the fibre next to it, and our object in drawing them back is to unhook these and cause them to re-lock themselves in a different position.

Now cut with the scissors close to the quill the quantity required, which for a trout fly would be about one-half of an inch, double it with the underpart of the feather *inside*. (See cut on next page).

Now grasp the fly with the thumb and finger of the left hand around the hackle, and close to where you desire to tie the wing on, place the wing in its proper position, (the point of which should reach to the end of the bend of the hook,) and grasp it firmly with the left hand, holding at the same time the hackles at the head of the fly down close to the body; now tie it down with three turns of your silk, do not loosen your hold on the feather until it has the three turns securely tied, then finish off with the invisible knot and varnish the head the same as previously directed.

TAILS.

When it is necessary to tie a tail on a fly proceed as directed for making hackles until you are ready to tie in the body; if the body is to be wrapped with tinsel make three or four turns of it around the shank of the hook and catch the

22   THE ART OF FLY TYING.

end of the tinsel with the plyers and let them hang. Now cut from the feather you desire to use for the tail two or three fibres from each side of the quill, place both *insides* together with the curve of the feather pointing up, convex side down, lay them on top of the hook, fasten with three turns of the tying silk on top of the wrapping you made in fastening on the tinsel, then proceed to tie in the hackle if it be a Palmer fly, or the body if not, and continue as before directed.

REVERSED WING FLIES.

To make reversed wing flies cut the feather the same as you would in making usual winged

flies, except that it requires to be longer. Snood the gut on the hook as usual and wind back spirally over the snooding with the wrapping silk to within one-eighth of an inch of the end of the hook. Now lay the wing which you have previously cut along the gut with the *convex side up* and with the butt ends of the feathers on top of the hook. (See cut.) Hold them in position by grasping them together with the hook between the thumb and finger of the left hand, take four turns of the wrapping silk around them, now cut off the surplus ends of the feathers on a bevel towards the point of the hook, this will give symmetry to the body of the fly. Then continue wrapping with the tying silk over the portion so cut, and from thence spirally to end of the wrapping on hook and proceed to tie in the tinsel, hackle, etc., exactly the same as if you were making a usual winged fly before described. After your fly is completed, except the wings, grasp them firmly with the right hand close to the head of the hook, pull the feathers outward and at the same time bending them back over the body of the fly. Now, with the left hand catch hold of the fly wings, and hackle, and tie over and over, close to the end of the bend of the wings with the wrapping silk, four turns, and finish off with the invisible knot.

Some fly-tyers, in place of using the invisible knot, leave one-sixty-fourth of an inch of the end of the hook bare after the wings of a fly are in position and are wrapped on, but not fastened off, and then bend the gut back over the wings. Now throw over the bare end of hook which was exposed by the bending back of the gut two or three half hitches of the silk and varnish it, this also makes a perfectly secure fastening.

Should you desire at any time to make the wings of a fly set up from the body, bend them back toward the gut, and before you have fastened them with the invisible knot, wind two or three turns of the tying silk around the body as close to the wings as possible; by this means you can make them set at any angle desired.

SCALE WING FLIES.

These, at times, are a very desirable fly, and are more nearly like the natural insect than wings made from feathers. I have found fish-scales taken from the shad to make the best wings. During the season collect as many scales as you desire, freshly taken from the fish, and dry them separately on blotting paper, as there is a mucilaginous substance adhering to them that, if they are allowed to dry in contact with each other it will cause them to adhere to one another. Cut from a piece of card board a pattern for the wing, which should be pear-shape with an elongated point. Lay this pattern on two or three of the dried scales and hold it in position with the plyers. You can then readily cut them the exact shape required.

When ready to tie in position on the fly, dip the points of the wings in water, which *immediately* causes them to become soft and pliable, and they can then be tied on precisely the same as a feather. These wings are very durable, as the property of softening as soon as water touches them prevents the fish from breaking them off.

SILK WORM GUT BODIES.

A fly made with this material is very durable and attractive. The gut can be colored any hade desired with "Diamond" dyes, after which the body of the fly should be wrapped with silk of the same color as the gut which you intend using. Soak the gut in warm water, tie it in and wrap it on over the silk body.

DYEING GUT.

The famous mist color for leaders and gut, for flies, is made as follows : Into an enameled boiler that will hold one pint, place as much best quality chip logwood as will go into a tea-spoon; fill the boiler with water and let it come to a boil. Allow it to boil for ten minutes, take it off the fire and place in it as much sulphate of iron as you can hold on a ten cent piece and stir it until dissolved. Now place the gut you desire to color in the liquor one and a half minutes, then if not dark enough insert it again, and allow it to stay until it has the desired shade.

The writer has used this recipe for years and has never found it injurious to the gut in any way.

COLORING FEATHERS.

Feathers for flies are always better in their natural colors, but there are some which it is desirable to use, more especially in hackles, which it is impossible to procure of the desired shade. As there is a natural oil in all feathers, and more especially in feathers from the duck and other water fowl, it must be removed before the dye will take effect on them. Tie in bunches of one or two dozen at the quill end and make a suds of soap and hot water; wash thoroughly and rinse in running water. Use "Diamond" dyes, which for this purpose I have found both good in color and permanent.

FLIES.

It now only remains to give a description of the flies most usually used, and if the foregoing directions have been carefully followed any one of the following can be readily tied. It would be well to remember that in using flies, the rule is on a dark day to use light colored flies and on a bright day, dark or more sombre colors. Of course this rule, like all others, has its exceptions.

The following are good at all seasons and at all stages of the water:

BROWN HACKLE AND BROWN PALMER.—Peacock herl body, tipped with tinsel, brown hackle.

RED HACKLE AND PALMER,—ALSO CALLED SOLDIER HACKLE.—Scarlet body ribbed with gold tinsel, fiery brown hackle.

BLACK HACKLE AND PALMER.—Black body ribbed with silver tinsel, or copper colored peacock herl tipped with tinsel. These are also tied with scarlet and with yellow bodies.

GRAY HACKLE AND PALMER.—Ash gray body ribbed with tinsel, gray, dominick or ash hackle. When the latter is used it is often called "ashey, ashey."

COACHMAN.—A good evening fly or on a dark day. Body, peacock herl tipped with tinsel, brown hackle, white wings.

ROYAL COACHMAN.—Body alternate rings of scarlet silk and peacock herl, tipped with tinsel, brown hackle, white wings. This fly is sometimes tied especially for bass, with a tail of barred wood duck or mottled mallard.

GRIZZLY KING.—Body dark green, ribbed with tinsel, gray hackle tied Palmer, tail scarlet Ibis wings mottled mallard.

QUEEN OF THE WATER.—Body orange, ribbed with tinsel, brown hackle tied Palmer, wings mottled mallard.

KING OF THE WATER.—Same as queen, but scarlet body, hackle *not* tied Palmer.

COW DUNG.—Body of yellow brown mohair or crewel, brown hackle, wings clay yellow chicken feather.

PROFESSOR.—Body yellow, ribbed with tinsel, brown hackle, tail scarlet Ibis, wings mottled mallard.

WHITE MILLER OR MOTH FLY.—Body white silk or chenille, tipped with tinsel; white hackle and wings.

SILVER BLACK.—Body black silk, ribbed with silver tinsel; gray hackle, black wings.

YELLOW SALLY.—Body yellow, ribbed with tinsel; hackle yellow, wings yellow.

GOVERNOR OR BROWN HEN.—Body of peacock herl, tipped with tinsel; brown hackle, mottled brown wings.

GREY COFFLIN.—Body grey, tipped with orange, hackle cinnamon color, tail two fibres from the mottled feather of the mallard, wings drab.

RED SPINNER.—Body wine colored silk, ribbed with tinsel; hackle brown, tail two fibres from a brown hackle, wings grey.

DARK STONE.—Body dark brown, hackle yellow, wings clay yellow.

SHOEMAKER.—Body grey, ribbed with orange; hackle light brown, tail mottled mallard, wings drab.

WHIRLING DUN.—Body dun color, hackle natural red, tail two fibres from mottled mallard, wings dun color.

BLACK GNATS AND MIDGES.

Body ostrich herl; if for a gnat, black hackle; if intended for a midge fly, use no hackle; wings drab.

SCARLET.—Body scarlet, hackle brown, tail three fibres from a brown hackle, wings brown.

BASS FLIES.

All the Palmers, and for Florida waters, yellow and green Palmer.

FERGUSON.—Body yellow, ribbed with tinsel; hackle light green, tail scarlet Ibis, wing wild turkey tail feather, with a strip of yellow on each side.

MONTREAL OR PORTLAND.—Body scarlet, ribbed with tinsel; hackle scarlet, tail Ibis; wings mottled brown, turkey tail.

BEE.—Body peacock herl, ribbed with yellow silk; hackle brown, wings turkey tail feathers.

ARMY WORM.—Body yellow, ribbed with green silk; hackle gray, tied Palmer and four strips of peacock herl drawn over the back and tied in at the head, no wings.

ACADEMY.—Body peacock herl, tipped with scarlet silk; hackle brown, tied Palmer; tail Ibis; wings brown, with a strip of Ibis on each side of them.

SELLERS.—Body scarlet, ribbed with tinsel; hackle brown, tied Palmer; wings and tail alternate strips of white, scarlet and black.

BLACK JUNE.—Body peacock herl, hackle black, wings black.

GOVERNOR ALVORD.—Body peacock herl, hackle red, wings, under wing cinnamon, upper wing black.

BLACK MOOSEHEAD.—Body black, ribbed with silver tinsel, tail green, hackle black, wings guinea.

The following are descriptions of natural flies which appear on small streams, as per Sarah McBride.

In April.

Black, gray, claret and scarlet, gnat, dark fox, blue blow, red fox, bright fox.

In May.

Black May, cow dung, great dun dotterel, dun, red spinner, yellow May, hod yellow dun, yellow Sally.

In June.

Hawthorn, shoemaker, black June, dark stone, green, brown and gray drake raven, wren fly, Stebbins.

In July.

Little egg lightning bug or firefly, little claret, fœted green.

In August, September.

Gray and brown cofflin, white miller.

The American Angler,

A WEEKLY JOURNAL, DEVOTED ENTIRELY TO

Fish, Fishing and Fish Culture,

The Only One in America.

Mr. SETH GREEN, the noted fishculturist, has charge of the Fish Culture department.

Send for Specimen Copy and Catalogue of Angling Literature—both free.

$3.00 per annum.

WM. C. HARRIS, Editor,
Office, 252 Broadway, New York.

Hinds' Black-Fly Cream,

FOR REPELLING
Black-Flies, Mosquitoes, Midges
AND OTHER INSECTS,
AND PROTECTING THE SKIN FROM
Sunburn, Irritation and Infection.

NO TAR.   **NO STAIN.**

Containing no Animal Fats.

Its efficacy *does not* depend upon Oil Pennyroyal alone (like most compounds,) and would be equally as effective without it. It washes off readily and leaves the skin soft, smooth and free from irritation.

Ladies may *safely* use it on the most delicate skin.

STATE OF MAINE.
OFFICE OF THE COMMISSIONER OF FISH AND GAME.

DIXFIELD, Feb. 25, 1883.

MR. A. S. HINDS, Portland.

I have used your "Black Fly Cream" and have found it a sure preventive against Flies and Mosquitoes: It is *neat* and *clean*. . . . .I should not think of going into the woods in Fly-time without it.

H. O. STANLEY.

CYNTHIANA, KY., April 23, 1883.

Please accept my thanks for the "Black-Fly Cream" received. It is the most elegant preparation for the purpose I have seen . . . . . . will take great pleasure in recommending it.

Yours very truly,

J. A. HENSHALL.

GLEN FALLS, VT., June 15, 1884.

MR. A. S. HINDS,

DEAR SIR:—For many years I have sought after *the* insect repellent and have tried all manner of compounds, but yours is the most thorough, at the same time cleanly, and not disagreeable.

Yours truly,

A. NELSON CHENEY.

PORTLAND, Feb., 27, 1883.

MR. A. S. HINDS,

DEAR SIR:—I used you "Black-Fly Cream" last season while trout fishing and found it a perfect success; was not troubled with Mosquitoes while using it. It is the *cleanest* and *best* preparation I ever used.

P. B. BURNHAM.

Price 25 cts. per Box, by mail 28 cts.

Sold by dealers in Sporting Goods.   Trade supplied by

A. B. SHIPLEY & SON, Phila.

Hotels and Routes for Sportsmen.

ASHLAND M.L.S. & W.R.Y. ROUTE.

Milwaukee, Lake Shore and Western Railway.

To the Best Fishing Resorts in the Northwest.

For Muskallonge and Black Bass.

The Eagle Waters, Twin Lakes, Lake St. Germaine, Tomahawk and Pelican Lakes.

For Brook Trout.

Watersmeet, Mich., The Ontonagon, Slate River, The Brule in Wis., and Brule in Mich., Gogebic Lake and Tributary Streams.

For Black Bass.

Gogebic Lake affords the best fishing in the country.

SPECIAL RATES FOR SPORTSMEN.

Address the undersigned for Guide Books and General information.

GEO. S. MARSH,
Gen'l Pass. and Ticket Agent, Milwaukee, Wis.

Trout Fishing,

Park House, Parkside, Pa.,

One mile from Henryville Station, D. L. & W.R.R.
90 miles from New York City,
100 miles from Philadelphia, via P. R. R.

The Finest Brook Trout Fishing in the Pocono Mountains,

Six Streams:

East and West Branch Broadheads, Cranberry, Heller, Paradise, Devil's Hole.

Good Gunning in October, November and December,

for

Pheasant, Quail, Rabbit and Squirrel.

For Particulars, address,

W. C. HENRY,
PARK SIDE,
Monroe Co.,
Pa.

A. B. SHIPLEY & SON'S Fly-Tyers' Cabinet.

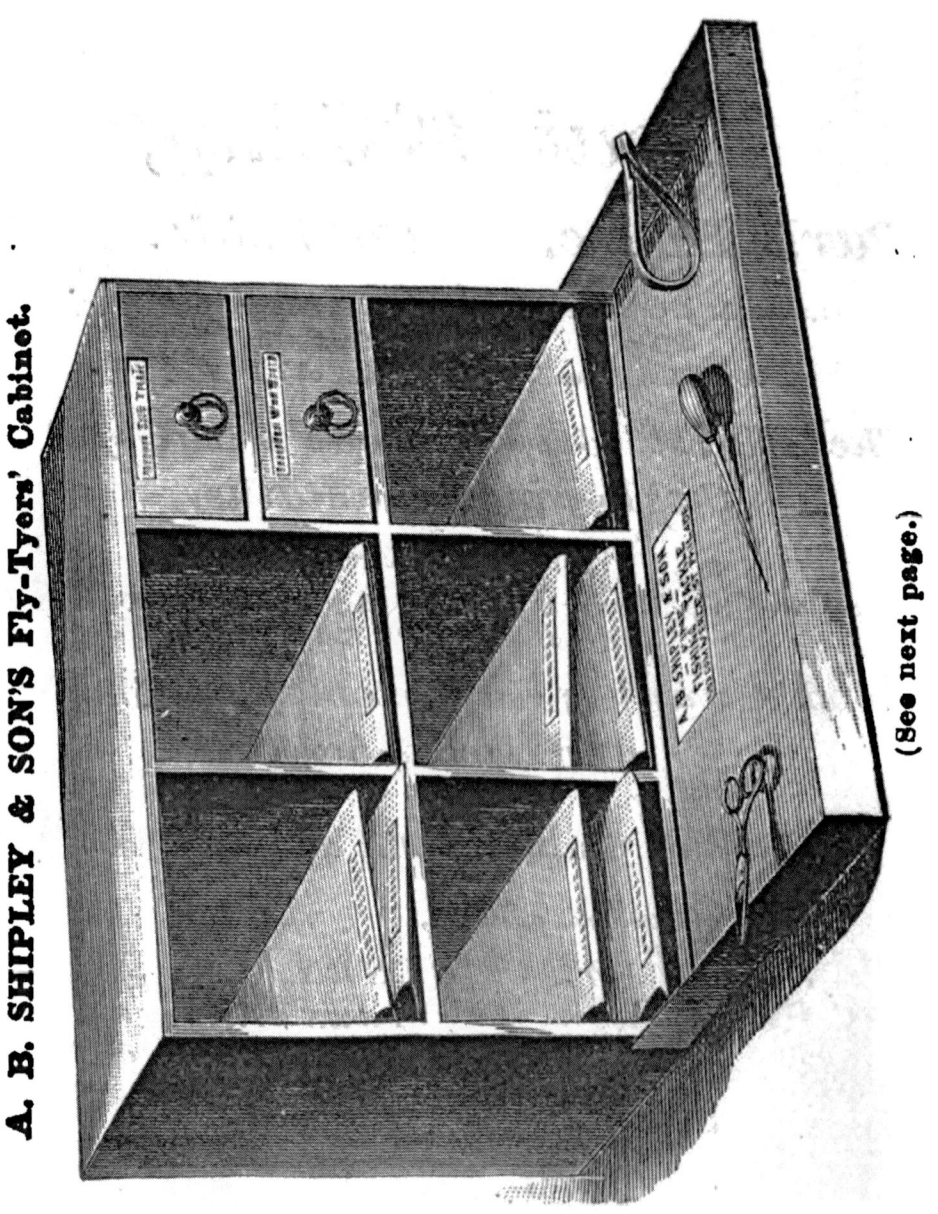

(See next page.)

Philadelphia Fishing Tackle House

MANUFACTURERS OF

Fine Fishing Tackle,

Rods, Lines, Reels, Flies, Shipley's Patent Fly-Books, &c.

Sole Agents for

Jno. James & Son's Celebrated Fish Hooks, &c.

Fly-Tyers' Cabinet,

Size, 12 x 8 inches.

Complete with Tools, Materials, &c.

Including this Book of Instructions

BY

M. A. SHIPLEY,

Price, $5.00.

A SPECIALTY OF THE

Celebrated Bethabara Wood

Fly and Bait Rods,

Stronger than Split Bamboo and as Tough and Elastic as Tempered Steel.

65 Page Illustrated Price List of Rods, Tackle, &c., 10 cts.

CPSIA information can be obtained
at www.ICGtesting.com
Printed in the USA
LVOW09s1836050218
565348LV00009B/559/P

9 781546 893295